I'm so proud of you Mum

I am so proud to have such a wonderful mum.

You are caring.

You are kind.

You have loved me since before I was even born.

I am so proud of the way you keep going.

Even on hard days, you get up,
and get on with whatever needs doing.

That takes strength.

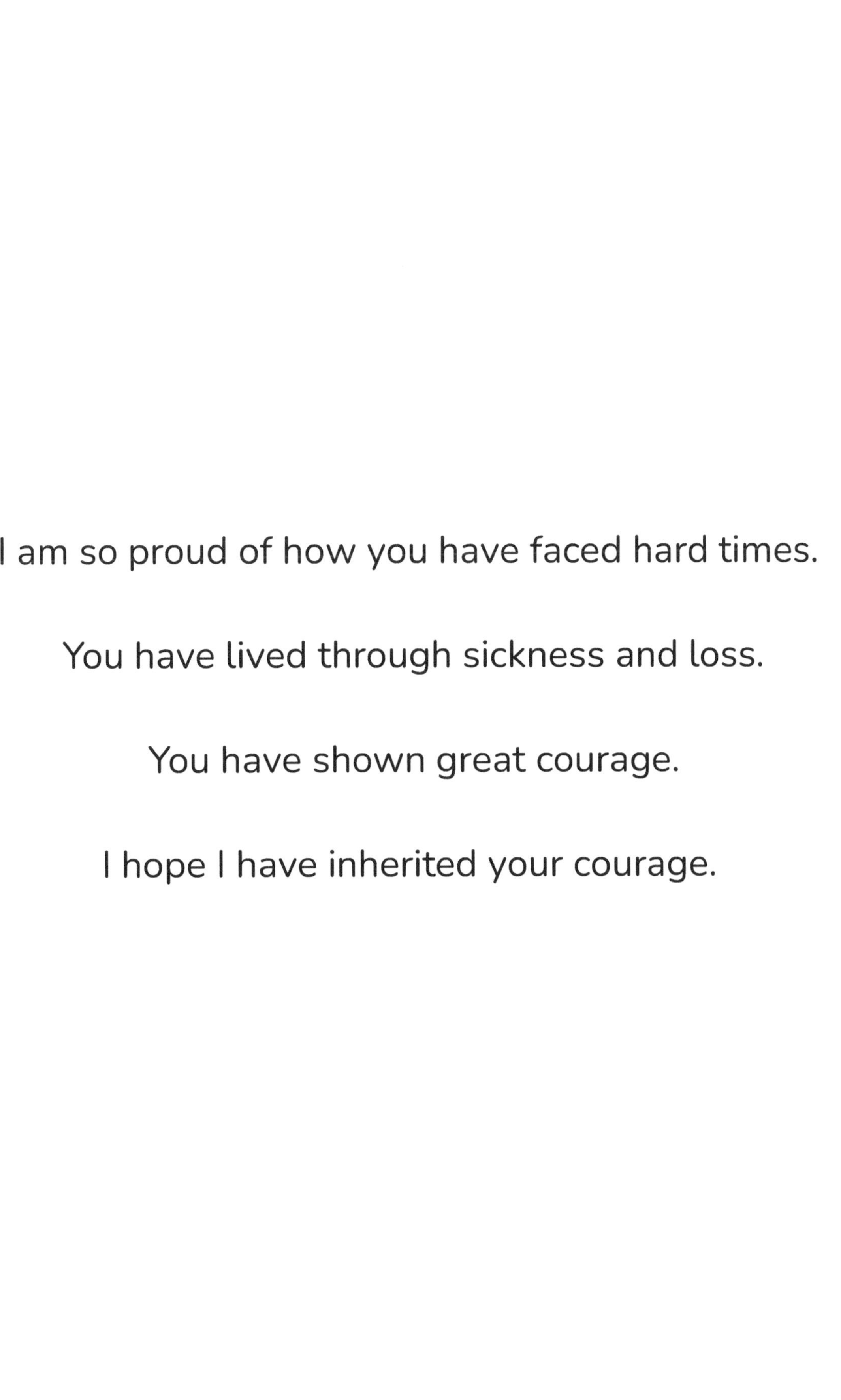

I am so proud of how you have faced hard times.

You have lived through sickness and loss.

You have shown great courage.

I hope I have inherited your courage.

I am so proud of how you have handled change.

A new home.

New routines.

New people.

That is a lot to cope with - and you do so with a brave face.

I am proud of the way you are letting others
help you.

You have always been the one to help
everyone else.

But now it is your turn to receive.

You are doing so well.

Looking back, I am so proud of your work and
your career.

You gave your best every day - sometimes in
difficult circumstances.

You made a difference in many people's lives.

I hope I am following in your footsteps.

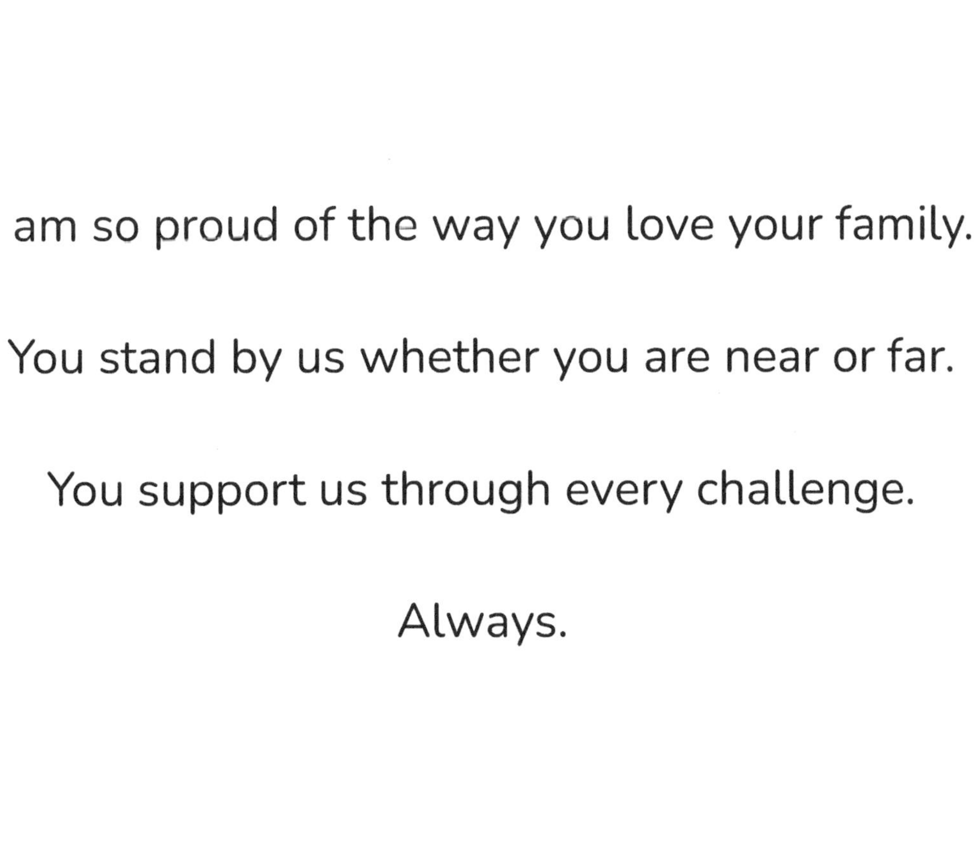

I am so proud of the way you love your family.

You stand by us whether you are near or far.

You support us through every challenge.

Always.

I am so proud of the home you made for us.

A home full of warmth.

Laughter.

And love for all the people and
pets who passed through.

I am so proud of your friendships.

You care so deeply about your friends.

And they care about you.

I am blessed to have learnt about the
importance of friendship from you.

I am so proud of the way you smile when
you see me walk through the door.

I know you see my big smile shining right
back at you.

I love the way we can sit and talk, passing
the time together without a care in the
world.

Looking back, I am so proud of how you
cared for your parents.

You were patient.

You were gentle.

You showed them love every day.

Now I am grown, I am in awe of all you did.

I am so proud of your wisdom.

You have taught me so much - about love, about commitment, about how to be the best person I can be.

I am still learning from you.

I am so proud of your compassion.

You see the good in people.

You care.

You show great patience and strength
when helping those in need.

You always have.

I am so proud of your loyalty.

To your family.

To your friends.

To the things you believe in.

I am so proud that you keep learning.

You stay curious.

You keep trying new things.

You have taught me what matters most.

Love.

Strength.

Kindness.

Family.

Friendship.

All of this is to say -
I am so proud of you, Mum!

And because I am like you in many ways...
I am proud of me too.

First published in 2026
ISBN: 978-1-7644353-1-4
Imprint: Bronwen Clark

Cover and interior design by Bronwen Clark
Images by Naris Artyeuenyong on Canva

Visit our website for more information: ww.dementiafriendlybooks.com

www.ingramcontent.com/pod-product-compliance
Lightning Source LLC
Chambersburg PA
CBHW042156030726
47599CB00004B/752